![DK] READERS

Level 3

Abraham Lincoln: Lawyer, Leader, Legend
Amazing Animal Journeys
Ant Antics
Ape Adventures
Beastly Tales
Bermuda Triangle
The Big Dinosaur Dig
Boys' Life: Ghost Stories
Boys' Life: Rapid Rescue
Disasters at Sea
Extreme Sports
George Washington: Soldier, Hero, President
Greek Myths
Helen Keller
Invaders from Outer Space
Plants Bite Back!
School Days Around the World
Shark Attack!
Space Heroes: Amazing Astronauts
Spacebusters: The Race to the Moon
Spiders' Secrets
Spies
The Story of Anne Frank
The Story of Chocolate
Tiger Tales
Titanic
Welcome to China
Fantastic Four: The World's Greatest
  Superteam
Indiana Jones: Great Escapes

The Invincible Iron Man: Friends and Enemies
LEGO® Friends: Friends Forever
LEGO® Friends: Summer Adventures
LEGO® Hero Factory: Heroes in Action
LEGO® Hero Factory: The Brain Wars
LEGO® Legends of Chima: The Race for CHI
LEGO® Monster Fighters: Watch Out, Monsters
  About!
Marvel Avengers: Avengers Assemble!
Marvel Heroes: Amazing Powers
Pokémon: Ash Battles his Rivals!
Pokémon: Legends of Sinnoh
Star Wars The Clone Wars: Ackbar's Underwater
  Army
Star Wars The Clone Wars: Forces of Darkness
Star Wars The Clone Wars: Jedi Heroes
Star Wars The Clone Wars: Yoda in Action!
Star Wars: The Battle for Naboo
Star Wars: Death Star Battles
Star Wars: Feel the Force!
Star Wars: I Want to Be a Jedi
Star Wars: The Legendary Yoda
Star Wars: Obi-Wan Kenobi, Jedi Knight
Star Wars: Star Pilot
Star Wars: The Story of Darth Vader
Wolverine: Awesome Powers
WWE: Kofi Kingston
WWE: The Big Show
WWE: Triple H
WWE: Undertaker

Level 4

Atlantis: The Lost City?
Boys' Life: Dangerous Beasts
Danger on the Mountain: Scaling the World's
  Highest Peaks
Days of the Knights
D-Day Landings: The Story of the Allied
  Invasion
Dinosaur Detectives
Dinosaurs! Battle of the Bones
Earthquakes and Other Natural Disasters
Extreme Machines
First Flight: The Story of the Wright Brothers
Flying Ace: The Story of Amelia Earhart
Free at Last! The Story of Martin Luther
  King, Jr.
Horse Heroes
Micro Monsters
Pirates! Raiders of the High Seas
Robin Hood
Secrets of the Mummies
Skate!
Snow Dogs: Racers of the North
The Story of Muhammad Ali
Thomas Edison: The Great Inventor
Volcanoes and Other Natural Disasters
Indiana Jones: The Search for Buried Treasure
LEGO® Friends: Welcome to Heartlake City
Marvel Avengers: World's Mightiest Super
  Hero Team

Marvel Heroes: Greatest Battles
Star Wars The Clone Wars: Jedi Adventures
Star Wars The Clone Wars: Planets in Peril
Star Wars: Beware the Dark Side
Star Wars: Darth Maul, Sith Apprentice
Star Wars: Epic Battles
Star Wars: Galactic Crisis!
Star Wars: Ultimate Duels
The Invincible Iron Man: The Rise of Iron Man
Wolverine: The Story of Wolverine

A Note to Parents

DK READERS is a compelling program for beginning readers, designed in conjunction with leading literacy experts, including Dr. Linda Gambrell, Distinguished Professor of Education at Clemson University. Dr. Gambrell has served as President of the National Reading Conference, the College Reading Association, and the International Reading Association.

Beautiful illustrations and superb full-color photographs combine with engaging, easy-to-read stories to offer a fresh approach to each subject in the series. Each DK READER is guaranteed to capture a child's interest while developing his or her reading skills, general knowledge, and love of reading.

The five levels of DK READERS are aimed at different reading abilities, enabling you to choose the books that are exactly right for your child:

Pre-level 1: Learning to read
Level 1: Beginning to read
Level 2: Beginning to read alone
Level 3: Reading alone
Level 4: Proficient readers

The "normal" age at which a child begins to read can be anywhere from three to eight years old. Adult participation through the lower levels is very helpful for providing encouragement, discussing storylines, and sounding out unfamiliar words.

No matter which level you select, you can be sure that you are helping your child learn to read, then read to learn!

LONDON, NEW YORK, MUNICH,
MELBOURNE, and DELHI

Editor Catherine Saunders
Designer Lisa Robb
Pre-Production Producer Marc Staples
Producer Louise Daly
Design Manager Nathan Martin
Publishing Manager Julie Ferris
Art Director Ron Stobbart
Publishing Director Simon Beecroft

Reading Consultant
Linda B. Gambrell, PH.D.

First American Edition, 2013
13 14 15 16 17 10 9 8 7 6 5 4 3 2 1
Published in the United States by DK Publishing
375 Hudson Street, New York, New York 10014

DK books are available at special discounts when purchased in
bulk for sales promotions, premiums, fund-raising, or
educational use.
For details, contact:
DK Publishing Special Markets
375 Hudson Street
New York, New York 10014
SpecialSales@dk.com

A catalog record for this book is available
from the Library of Congress.

ISBN: 978-1-4654-0263-9 (Paperback)
ISBN: 978-1-4654-0264-6(Hardcover)

Printed and bound in China by L. Rex

Discover more at
www.dk.com
www.LEGO.com

Contents

4   Alpha 1 Team

6   Community relations

8   Ready for action

12   Dangerous mission

14   Brainy beasts

20   Factory attack!

22   Furno XL vs. Pyrox

24   Stormer vs. Frost Beast

26   Bulk vs. Bruizer

28   Breez vs. Ogrum

30   Rocka vs. Scarox

32   Evo vs. Aquagon

34   Surge's mission

36   Brain popping

38   Deadly enemy

40   Secret weapon

42   Rocka vs. Dragon Bolt

44   Hero in trouble

46   Back to normal

48   Glossary

DK READERS

READING
3
ALONE

LEGO HERO FACTORY

The Brain Wars

Written by Catherine Saunders

Alpha 1 Team

Preston Stormer and his team are the toughest heroes the Hero Factory has ever built. These brave heroes are smart, strong, and highly skilled. Together, they are known as Alpha 1 Team, and they have saved the galaxy from Von Nebula, Fire Lord, Witch Doctor, Voltix, Black Phantom, and many other evil villains.

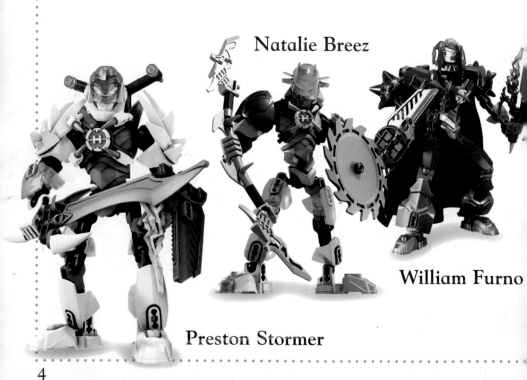

Natalie Breez

William Furno

Preston Stormer

Hero Cuffs

Every hero carries Hero Cuffs. Captured villains are cuffed and then taken away to the Villain Storage Unit in the Hero Factory.

The team works together to defeat its enemies. So far, Alpha 1 Team has never failed in a mission. But the heroes are about to face a truly evil enemy. Who will win this battle?

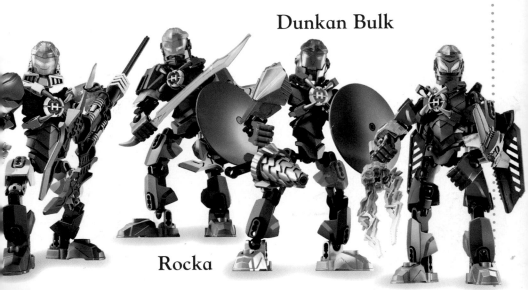

Dunkan Bulk

Rocka

Nathan Evo

Mark Surge

Community relations

There is more to being a hero than capturing villains. The robot heroes train hard to prepare themselves for missions. They learn how to use lots of different weapons and develop new battle tactics.

It's also important to get to know the citizens that the robot heroes are built to protect. So, whenever they can, Alpha 1 Team spends time meeting the good people of Makuhero City. The heroes sign autographs, answer questions, and show off some of their skills. The citizens love it! It's so exciting to meet the brave heroes who work so hard to protect them.

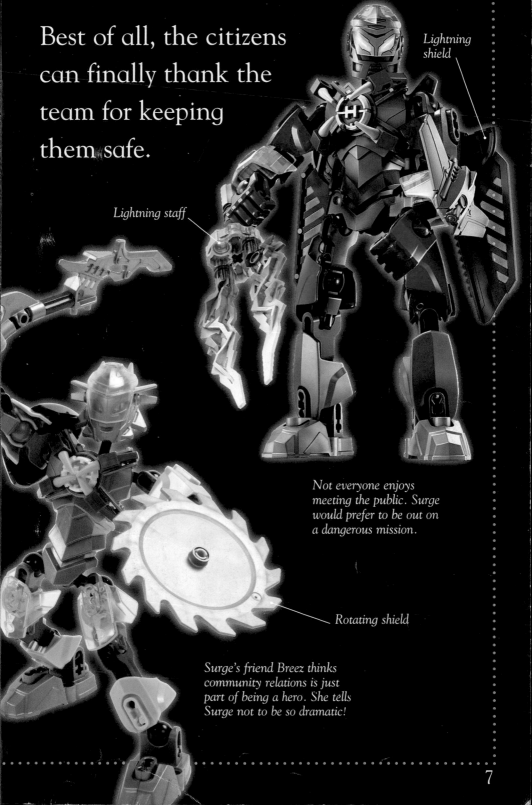

Best of all, the citizens can finally thank the team for keeping them safe.

Lightning shield

Lightning staff

Not everyone enjoys meeting the public. Surge would prefer to be out on a dangerous mission.

Rotating shield

Surge's friend Breez thinks community relations is just part of being a hero. She tells Surge not to be so dramatic!

Ready for action

Alpha 1 Team likes to stay one step ahead of its foes so the heroes always carry the best weapons. It is Mission Manager Zib and his assistant Quadal's job to upgrade the heroes' weapons.

Fire sword

Hero visor

Shoulder armor

Fire shield

Hero Core gives the Hero life

Furno XL

Zib says it's time for another weapons upgrade. All the heroes will be fitted with new equipment. Furno is first in line. Every hero receives a new visor, but Furno also gets a Fire Shield and a Fire Sword. These mighty weapons can withstand the hottest temperatures without melting.

Fire Sword

Fire Shield

New Hero Clamp
Inside each hero is a Hero Core, which gives it life. Now the Core is protected by a tough new Clamp.

Furno is not the only one with new equipment. Team leader Stormer has a new Ice Blade and Ice Deflector, while Surge receives a Lightning Staff and Lightning Shield. Evo gets propellers and a pincer weapon, and Bulk has a Laser Drill and Missile Launcher. Rocka's new weapons include a Shovel Shield and a long Dyna-Lance. He has also been given a top-secret piece of equipment, but he is not ready to show it to the team yet. Last in line is Breez, who can't wait to try out her new weapons.

Rocka's new
Dyna-Lance

Breez's new staff is made from wood and has four sharp steel blades. She will need to practice using it.

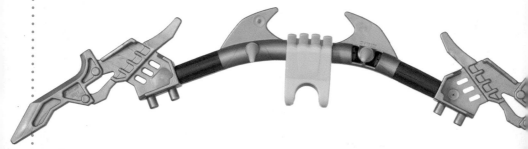

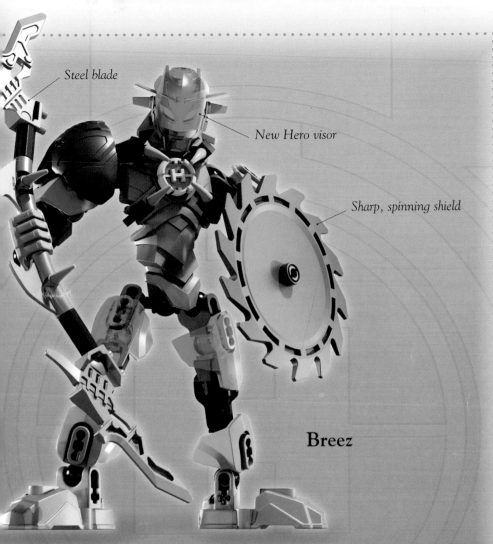

Steel blade

New Hero visor

Sharp, spinning shield

Breez

Breez receives a Spinning Shield Blade and a sharp Wood-Steel Staff. Only a foolish villain would mess with her!

This Spinning Shield Blade can be used at close range, or thrown for long-range attacks.

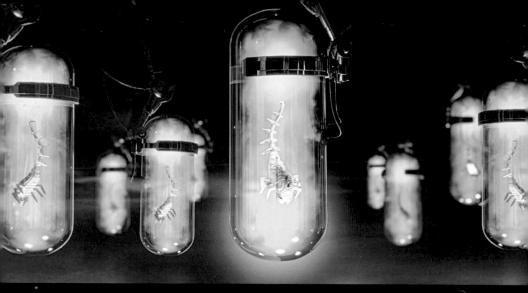

Dangerous mission

Alpha 1 Team has defeated many enemies, but in a far corner of the galaxy a new foe is planning an attack. In a secret lab, there are rows and rows of jars, each containing a slimy creature. Take a closer look— they're not creatures, they're Brains!

Someone evil is controlling the Brains, and now this mysterious mastermind wants to send them to the Hero Factory. Watch out Alpha 1 Team, here comes trouble!

Using individual mini-spacecraft, the unknown villain transports the Brains all around the galaxy. When they land, the Brains carry out the first part of their orders: Find a strong host creature, and take control of it.

Brainy beasts

Surely a tiny Brain is no match for a huge beast! Unfortunately, evil Brains beat brawn every time. Even a mighty ogre can't fight off an evil Brain. The swamp-dwelling Ogrum is one of the Brain's first victims.

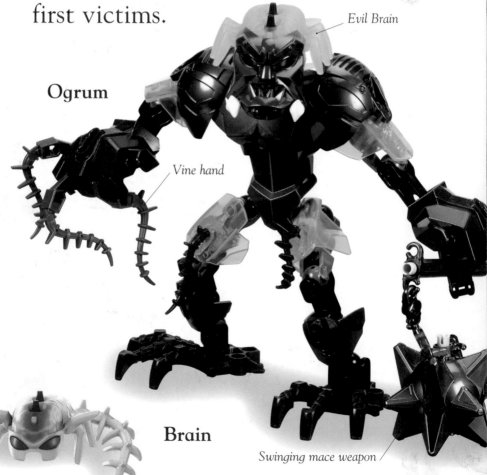

Evil Brain

Ogrum

Vine hand

Brain

Swinging mace weapon

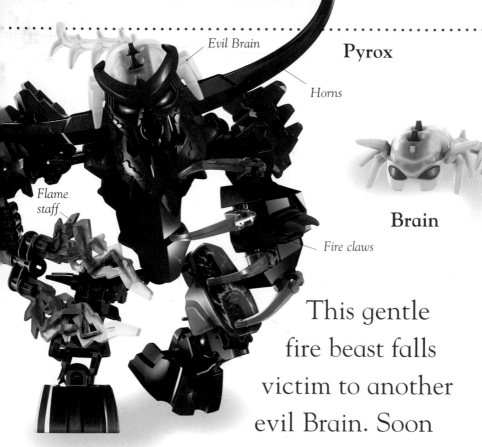

Evil Brain

Horns

Pyrox

Flame staff

Fire claws

Brain

This gentle fire beast falls victim to another evil Brain. Soon the Brain has control of Pyrox's fiery powers. These include the ability to shoot flames from his arms and make his body super hot.

Brain control
The Brains take control of their victims by attaching themselves to their heads. When the creature's eyes glow red, the Brain has it under its control.

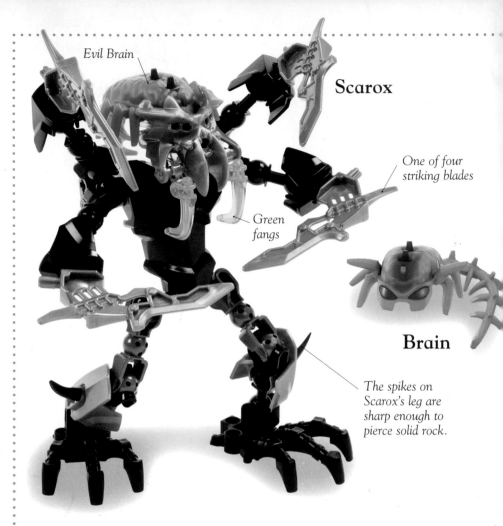

Evil Brain

Scarox

One of four
striking blades

Green
fangs

Brain

The spikes on
Scarox's leg are
sharp enough to
pierce solid rock.

One evil Brain travels to the hot
desert to find a host creature. Scarox
is tough enough to survive in the
scorching sand, but he cannot shake
off the Brain. Soon the Brain has
Scarox under its control. It directs
him to Makuhero City.

Brains are not too fond of freezing temperatures, but the icy area of the galaxy is worth a trip. Here, an evil Brain finds a powerful victim— Frost Beast. This icy creature has freezing breath and a range of deadly ice weapons. Frost Beast can't resist the Brain's attack, and he becomes another host.

Evil Brain

Frost Beast

Brain

Shovel weapon

Ice claws

Another Brain lands in the sea.
There it finds a shy beast hiding
behind a coral reef because he is
scared of the other ocean creatures.
Aquagon soon falls victim to the evil
Brain—and he is transformed from
timid to terrifying! Aquagon's mission
will take him far from the ocean.

Evil Brain

Aquagon

Shoulder spike

Double-bladed
weapon

Brain

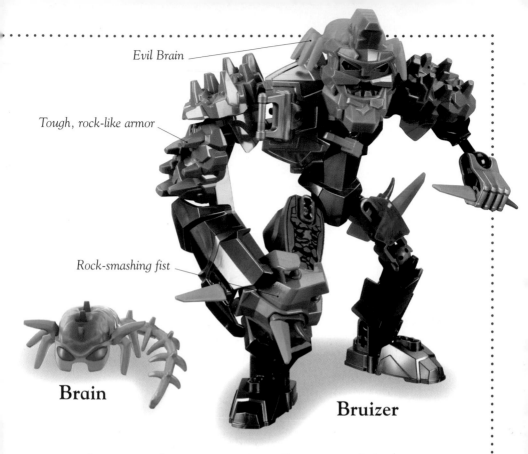

Evil Brain

Tough, rock-like armor

Rock-smashing fist

Brain

Bruizer

This rock giant prefers making
sculptures to breaking rocks.
However, when an evil Brain takes
control of him, Bruizer smashes
everything in sight. And he enjoys it!

The Brains' last victim is hiding in
a dark cave. This huge, scary beast
has awesome powers. And he's
heading for the Hero Factory...

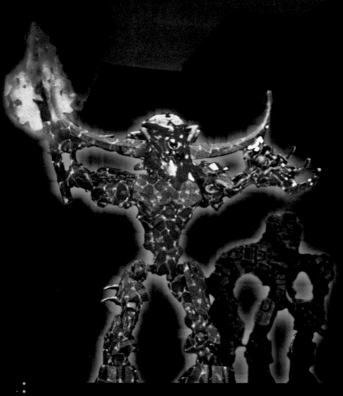

These creatures are not evil, but the Brains who control them are. The poor beasts have no idea what they are doing.

Factory attack!

The evil Brains have traveled all over the galaxy finding thousands of innocent creatures to control. Now they are ready to carry out the second part of their orders—launch a massive attack on the Hero Factory!

The Brains found the first part of their mission easy, but the second part will be tougher. Alpha 1 Team will do whatever it takes to defend the Hero Factory. Equipped with their new, upgraded gear, Stormer, Furno, Surge, Evo, Breez, Rocka, and Bulk are prepared for their most dangerous mission yet. It's heroes vs. Brains!

At first the team doesn't understand why the creatures are attacking them.

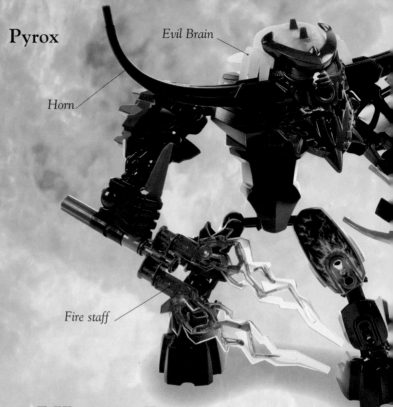

Pyrox

Evil Brain

Horn

Fire staff

Furno XL vs. Pyrox

Thousands of Brain-controlled creatures have arrived in Makuhero City and they are heading toward the Hero Factory. The beasts create damage, destruction, and danger wherever they go. Furno and Alpha 1 Team are determined to protect the citizens of Makuhero City.

With his new Fire Sword and Fire Shield at the ready, Furno decides to take on Pyrox and any other fire beasts out there. It's the hottest battle Furno has ever known!

Fire Sword

Cloak

Furno

Stormer vs. Frost Beast

Stormer wants to find a way to defeat the Brains without harming the creatures underneath. However, it won't be easy—the powerful Brain-controlled creatures are attacking him and his team! The heroes need to hold them off long enough to find a solution.

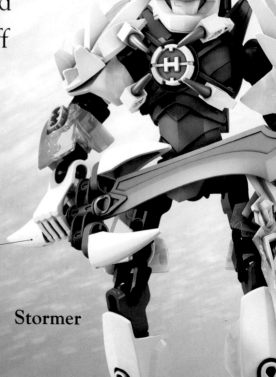

Ice Blade

Stormer

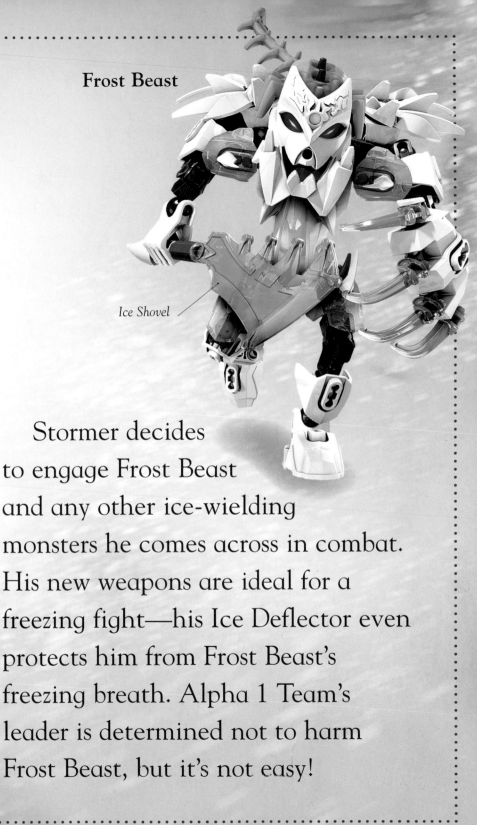

Frost Beast

Ice Shovel

Stormer decides to engage Frost Beast and any other ice-wielding monsters he comes across in combat. His new weapons are ideal for a freezing fight—his Ice Deflector even protects him from Frost Beast's freezing breath. Alpha 1 Team's leader is determined not to harm Frost Beast, but it's not easy!

Bulk vs. Bruizer

Bulk is the biggest hero in Alpha 1 Team, but Bruizer is even bigger. The rock giant, and others like him, are smashing, bashing, and crashing their way toward the Hero Factory. Bulk is going to need all his energy for this battle!

Drill cutter and Missile Launcher

Bulk

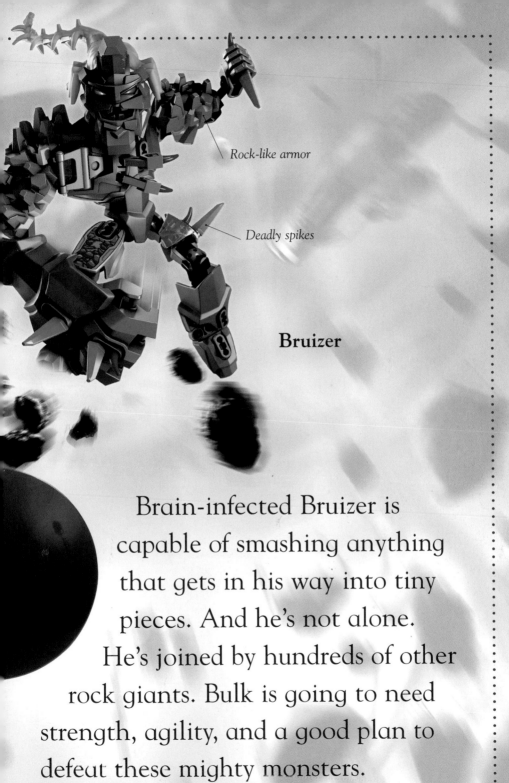

Rock-like armor

Deadly spikes

Bruizer

Brain-infected Bruizer is capable of smashing anything that gets in his way into tiny pieces. And he's not alone. He's joined by hundreds of other rock giants. Bulk is going to need strength, agility, and a good plan to defeat these mighty monsters.

Breez vs. Ogrum

Breez's new weapons are perfect for slicing through vines, so she seeks out Ogrum and all the other Brain-controlled swamp beasts. Breez hopes that she won't need to use her weapons on Ogrum. She has the ability to communicate with most creatures and would rather negotiate than fight. Unfortunately, Breez's skill doesn't work when the creature is being controlled by a Brain!

Deadly weapon
Ogrum creates his mace weapon by bashing a rock into a spiked shape and adding a vine chain. He can swing it at his foes.

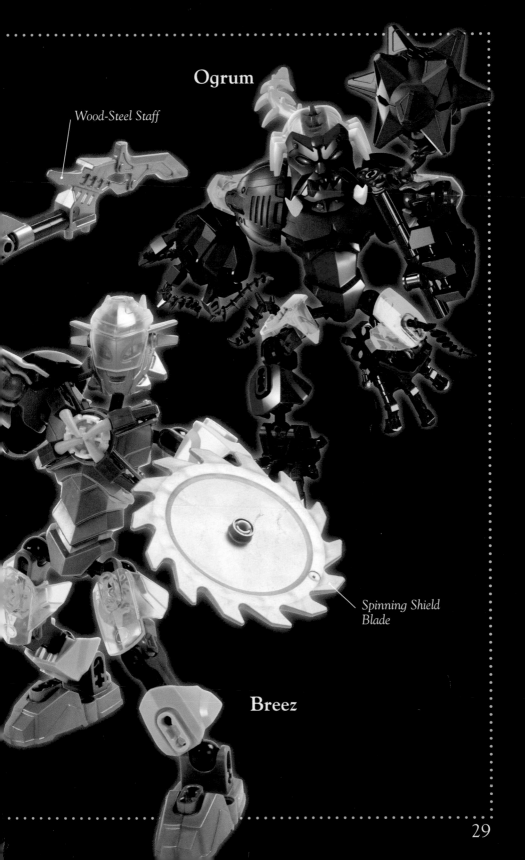

Ogrum

Wood-Steel Staff

Spinning Shield
Blade

Breez

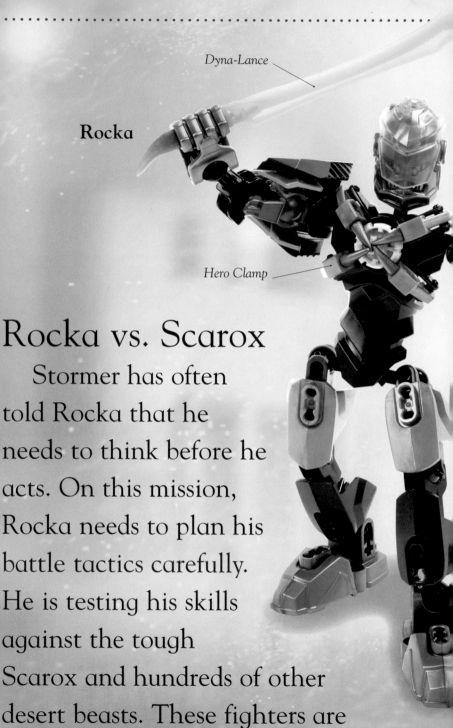

Dyna-Lance

Rocka

Hero Clamp

Rocka vs. Scarox

Stormer has often told Rocka that he needs to think before he acts. On this mission, Rocka needs to plan his battle tactics carefully. He is testing his skills against the tough Scarox and hundreds of other desert beasts. These fighters are fast, and wield sharp striking blades.

Scarox

Green fang

Striking blade

Scarox has another big
advantage over Rocka—he has six
limbs but the robot hero only has
four! Rocka will need to think
and act quickly to defeat this foe. He
certainly doesn't plan to let it get
close enough to use its fangs.

Evo vs. Aquagon

Although Aquagon is a sea creature, he proves to be quite dangerous on land, too. Thanks to the evil Brain controlling him, the formerly shy sea beast is on a rampage in Makuhero City.

Sharp blade

Aquagon

Evo knows he will need speed and good aim to catch this slippery creature, and the hundreds like him on the loose. Evo has been practicing with his new pincer weapon and can throw it with deadly accuracy.

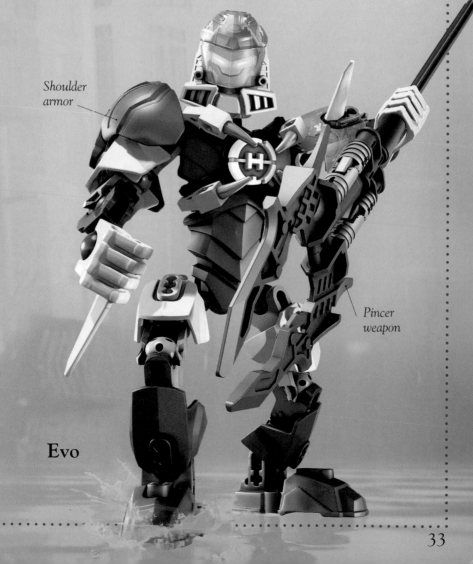

Shoulder armor

Pincer weapon

Evo

Hero visor

Lightning Shield

Lightning Staff

Surge

Surge's mission

Surge wanted an exciting new mission, and he's certainly got one! His job is to protect the entrance to the Hero Factory from the Brains.

At first Surge does well. He manages to fight off hundreds of the Brain-controlled creatures. But the Brains are sneakier than he thought. A cunning Brain attacks Surge from above and lands on his head.
The hero tries to shake him off but the evil Brain is too strong for him. Now Surge is infected, too!

The Brain-controlled robot hero abandons his mission. With glowing red eyes, he heads back into the Hero Factory. Will Alpha 1 Team be able to stop Surge before the evil Brain makes him do something terrible?

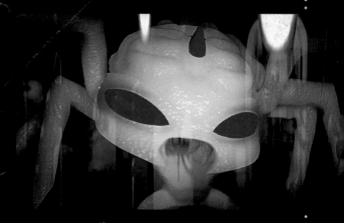

Brain popping

The Brain-controlled Surge is on the loose in the Hero Factory, but the rest of Alpha 1 Team has no idea. The team is busy battling all the other Brains and trying not to hurt the creatures underneath.

Finally, Bulk hits upon the answer to this problem.

High Impact Hero Shield

Bulk

Bulk and the team pop as many Brains as they can. As soon as the Brains let go of the creatures, the team arrests the evil aliens and sends the poor beasts home.

When Bulk bashes the Brain's second red spike, it lets go of its creature. All Alpha 1 Team has to do now is hit all the Brains on their weak spots. That's the easy part. The hard part is getting close enough to make a hit!

Weak spot
Even evil Brains have a weak spot. And now the robot heroes know how to hit them where it hurts!

Second spike

Deadly enemy

Since Surge has mysteriously disappeared, Furno orders Rocka to guard the entrance to the Hero Factory instead. Rocka is happy to help, but he wonders where Surge has gone.

Meanwhile, the rest of the team might have found the secret to defeating the Brains, but their problems are not over yet. The heroes are about to meet the big Dragon Bolt!

This huge but harmless dragon was minding his own business in his cave when an evil Brain attacked him. Even the mighty Dragon Bolt couldn't resist the Brain's power and was soon under its control.

Wing

Dragon Bolt is not only bigger and more powerful than the other creatures, he can also fly. Although Rocka is guarding the entrance to the Hero Factory, he can't stop Dragon Bolt. The dragon flies in and enters via the roof!

Evil Brain

Lightning bolt

Tail

Dragon claw

Dragon Bolt

Secret weapon

Mission Control Manager Zib finally locates Surge. He notifies Alpha 1 Team that the rogue robot hero is on the loose and he must be stopped. Rocka volunteers to take care of Dragon Bolt while the other heroes go and rescue Surge.

However, Rocka soon discovers that stopping Dragon Bolt and popping the Brain won't be easy. Whenever the hero gets close to Dragon Bolt, the Brain-controlled creature flies away! Worse still, Dragon Bolt's Lightning weapons are blasting holes all over the Hero Factory. Suddenly, Rocka has an idea: It's time to reveal his new, top-secret equipment—it's a jet pack!

Tracking device

Missile launchers

Jet pack

Jet boosters

Movable wings

Rocka

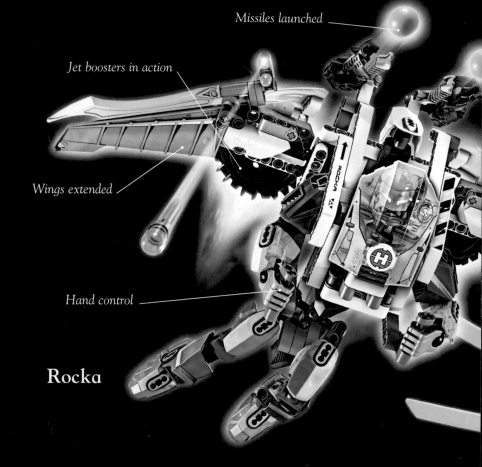

Missiles launched

Jet boosters in action

Wings extended

Hand control

Rocka

Rocka vs. Dragon Bolt

Rocka straps on his jet pack and activates it. Now he can fly, too! It's time to pop that evil Brain before Dragon Bolt and his Lightning weapons destroy the Hero Factory.

In an epic aerial battle, Dragon Bolt puts up a brave fight, but Rocka is too smart for him. He uses the jet pack to get close to the Brain-infected beast and then switches it to autopilot. Then, Rocka unstraps the jet pack and leaps onto the dragon's back. Rocka pops the Brain and releases Dragon Bolt.

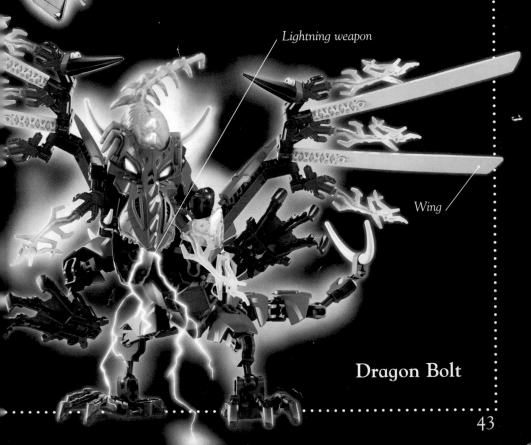

Lightning weapon

Wing

Dragon Bolt

Hero in trouble

While Rocka is taking care of Dragon Bolt, the rest of Alpha 1 Team hunt for Surge. The heroes find him in the Assembly Tower— the place where robot heroes are built. The Brain-infected hero has been busy. He has built an army of generic robots. Was this the Brain's evil plan all along?

This is the Mission Control Room, where Zib and Quadal monitor all the action. From here they can track all the heroes and also communicate with them.

The team works out a plan. Furno, Stormer, Bulk, and Evo attack the army of generic robots while Breez tries to save her friend. She tells Surge that he must fight the Brain. Her words seem to reach Surge and he pauses just long enough for Breez to pop the Brain.

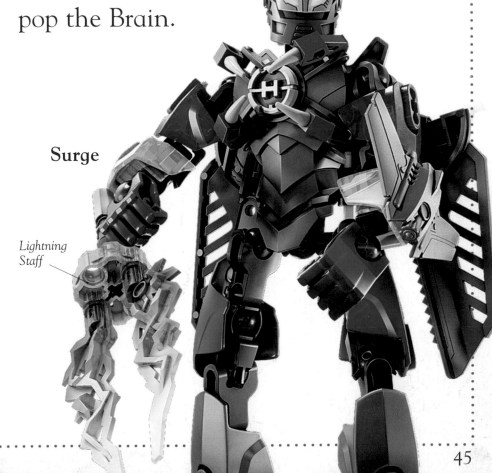

Surge

Lightning Staff

Back to normal

With Surge back to being a hero, Alpha 1 Team quickly defeats the rest of the Brains. The Brains are imprisoned in the Villain Storage Unit and the creatures they infected return home safely. The Hero Factory is secure and Makuhero City is a peaceful place once more.

Surge has learned two important things during this adventure: He'll never complain again, and he will always listen to his friend Breez!

The end?

The heroes think that they have all the Brains safely locked up in the Villain Storage Unit. But have they really got them all?

Glossary

Autograph
A handwritten signature. The citizens of Makuhero City collect autographs of the robot heroes to prove they have met them.

Blade
The flat, sharp cutting part of a sword.

Brawn
Strong muscles. The intelligent Brains are able to outwit the creatures they attack despite the creatures' brawn.

Citizen
A person who lives in Makuhero City.

Close range
Very nearby.

Combat
A fight or battle between two opponents.

Enemy
Someone who is hostile to someone or something.

Equipment
The things needed for a task or job.

Fangs
Long, sharp teeth through which poisonous venom is injected into victims.

Foe
Another word for enemy.

Galaxy
A large system of stars and planets.

Hero
Someone admired for his or her brave deeds.

Jet pack
A jet-powered backpack.

Lab
Short for laboratory, a lab is where science experiments are carried out.

Lightning
An electric spark of light.

Mission
An important task or duty. The robot heroes go on missions to defeat dangerous enemies.

Negotiate
To reach an agreement through discussion.

Ogre
A giant monster.

Solution
The answer to a problem.

Tactics
Plans and methods used in battle.

Timid
Shy and afraid. Aquagon was a timid creature before the evil Brain took control of its body.

Upgrade
A new, improved version of something.

Victim
Someone who suffers harm at the hands of another. The beasts were victims of the evil Brains.

Villain
An evil character. The hero robots defeat the evil Brains villians.

Index

Alpha 1 Team 4, 5,
    6, 8, 12, 21, 22, 25,
    26, 35, 36, 37, 40,
    44, 46
Aquagon 18, 32
Assembly Tower 44
Brains 12, 13, 14, 32,
    34, 35, 36, 37, 38,
    40, 42, 43, 44, 45,
    46, 47
Breez 4, 7, 10, 11, 21,
    28, 45, 47
Bruizer 19, 26, 27
Bulk 5, 10, 21, 26, 27,
    36, 37, 44
Citizens 6, 7
Dragon Bolt 38, 39,
    40, 42, 43, 44
Dyna-Lance 10
Evo 5, 10, 21, 32, 33,
    45
Fire Shield 9, 23
Fire Sword 9, 23
Furno 4, 9, 10, 21, 22,
    23, 38, 45
Galaxy 4, 12, 13, 20
Hero Clamp 9, 30
Hero Core 9
Hero Cuffs 5
Hero Factory 4, 12,
    20, 21, 22, 26,
    34, 35, 36, 38, 39,
    40, 46
Hero Visor 9, 11, 34

Host creature 13
Ice Beast 17, 24, 25
Ice Blade 10
Ice Deflector 10, 25
Jet pack 40, 43
Laser Drill 10
Lightning Shield 10,
    11, 34
Lightning Staff 7, 10,
    34
Mace weapon 28
Makuhero City 6, 22,
    32, 46
Missile Launcher 10
Mission 21, 34
Ogrum 14, 28
Pincer weapon 10, 33
Propellers 10
Pyrox 15, 22, 23
Quadal 8
Rocka 5, 10, 21,
    30, 38, 39, 40, 42,
    43, 44
Rock giants 27
Scarox 16, 30
Shield 7
Shovel Shield 10
Spinning Shield Blade
    11, 29
Stormer 4, 10, 21, 24,
    30, 45
Surge 5, 7, 10, 21, 34,
    35, 36, 38, 40, 44,
    45, 46, 47

Villain Storage Unit
    46, 47
Weapons 6, 8, 9, 25,
    28
Wood-Steel Staff 11,
    29
Zib 8, 40